MW00609065

This book is a gift from:
Down Syndrome Association Of Central Kentucky
P.O. Box 910516, Lexington, KY 40591-0516
859-494-7809
www.dsack.org

Every reasonable effort has been made to identify and contact individuals photographed.
Errors or omissions will be corrected in subsequent editions.

Publisher: Art of Possibility Press, Seaman, Ohio
Printed in the United States

To inquire about additional copies of this book or for permission to reproduce any material
in this book, please contact the author at:

1115 Lori Lane
Westerville, Ohio 43081
bmckenzie@columbus.rr.com

Reflections of Erin

The Importance of Belonging, Relationships, and Learning *with* Each Other

By Barbara McKenzie
Design by Chris McKenzie

Acknowledgments

To my daughter Erin – You have made such a difference in my life and, I have happily discovered, in the lives of many others. I love you and miss you.

To my husband Gary – I have loved and admired you since we first met in 1967. Thank you for always giving me your trust and support, even when you haven't been quite sure what I was thinking. You are one of the most caring and committed people I know, and I am lucky to share my life with you.

To my son Chris – My love for you is huge, but hopefully not stifling. Thank you for never being afraid to share your honest perspective and creativity.

To my friend Candee – Thank you for being there to help me think through all this and for being such a good friend.

To Erin's friends – Thank you for your unconditional love for Erin, your caring support of our family, and for continuing to keep Erin's spirit and the vision of welcoming, inclusive communities alive.

To Erin's teachers – Thank you for taking risks, collaborating with our family and each other, discovering Erin's strengths and gifts, nurturing her interests, and expanding her opportunities.

To everyone who contributed photographs, reviewed drafts, and offered suggestions – Thank you for your time, thoughtful responses, and inspiration.

*This book is dedicated
to the loving grandparents of
Erin Virginia McKenzie*

*Grammy and Grandpa McKenzie
and
Grandpa Contak*

*And to Grandma Virginia Contak, whom Erin never got
to know but was named after.*

Prologue

Our daughter Erin unexpectedly passed away just two months after graduating from high school in 2004. Her sudden death brought forth a multitude of people, each expressing how he or she had been personally transformed by Erin's presence and full participation in school and in life. Throughout her life, I shared stories, observations, surprises, and my reflections about what I felt we were learning from Erin and the relationships she and we were building. Some of those stories and photographs are gathered in this book.

I did choose to highlight the good news rather than the bad. Maybe I saw it as a way to keep the positive energy going for me and those with whom I was sharing. If I had dwelled on all the effort it took and the barriers our family encountered, I'm not sure it would have helped any of us. More importantly, Erin might not have had the opportunity to have the happy, *ordinary* life she enjoyed—although for too short a time.

Our vision for Erin was…

…That she would have a life in a community that values diversity and accentuates strengths and the opportunity to share her gifts and talents with that community

…That she would have reciprocal relationships with friends who would encourage her to experience new things and to communicate and advocate for herself

…That she would have the same opportunities to learn and participate in typical classroom, extracurricular, and community activities when they would typically happen, graduate from high school with her class in 2004, and have continued educational opportunities in college and a career that interests her

It all happened. She was even happily beginning to be a part of her next community by doing something she loved with the Theatre Department at Otterbein College.

My good friend Candee Basford often ponders through her journaling, art work, and in conversation with others, how to change the world and build welcoming and inclusive communities. The best way I know how to try and do that is by celebrating Erin's life and reflecting on what we've learned from her and those we've met on this journey. My hope is that we will discover our gifts and embrace our interdependence—our need to learn *with* each other.

Act I – Discovering

Inclusion Is Really Good Teaching, Not Special Teaching

Original Version Written Winter 1992

A year ago we were beginning our discussions with school personnel concerning our desire to have our daughter totally included in the same elementary school her brother attends. This is not an exclusive private school—just a public school that happens to be in our neighborhood. All the other children who live in our area go to it unless their parents have made private choices. Then why did we need to have several meetings to decide if our daughter would be "allowed" to attend this school?

Our daughter has one of those labels that the state and federal government say make her eligible for special education services. The label that has been given to her by the professionals is cognitive or developmental disability. The assumption is that if our daughter is put into a special classroom for students with the same label, then she can be made ready to rejoin her community in controlled increments at a later date.

Since our daughter was never made ready to join our family and was an equal, fully participating member from the day she was born, that idea seemed strange. So we decided to pursue a different option—inclusion. That brings us back to the reason for all the meetings.

Fortunately our school district employs some innovative and caring individuals who have been willing to take a risk, be creative, bend the rules, and do what is right. Together we have worked on a vision of how things could be.

This has not been an easy process. It is difficult to leave old "good ideas" to explore new dreams and possibilities. Job descriptions have needed to change. Some well-meaning people have not wanted to give up control of our daughter. Natural inclusion that may be enhanced and supported is much different from the old idea of controlled mainstreaming based on perceived ability. We have all learned a lot, especially our daughter.

Inclusion as it applies to education requires flexibility, creativity, cooperative theories, collaboration, commitment, and risk—all of the requirements of good teaching, not special teaching. It's about adults supporting other adults and children; children supporting other children and adults; and everyone learning how to problem-solve together. It's about discovering the strengths and gifts in each of us.

Discussions have begun again for next year, but they are not about whether or not our daughter will be allowed to attend our neighborhood school and be in the class she would be in if no label existed. Our daughter is welcome at her neighborhood school. She will be following her classmates and friends to the next grade; will hopefully have unlimited opportunities to learn; will receive supports when needed from adults, peers, and technology; and will be able to offer her own talents to share with and to teach others.

"Inclusion does not require special skills; rather it is based on unconditional love and respect for each person's gifts."

Gathering Community

When planning Erin's 10th birthday, we had a "pre-party" planning party with a few of her friends. Not only did the girls come up with some great ideas, but they also made sure that Erin was included in all the planning. While I wanted to pick their brains, they wanted to make sure that Erin had a say in what was decided and often reminded me of that.

The theme was *The Lion King*, the popular movie that year. ALL the girls drew pictures to describe the activities chosen. Dunking for apples was "Eating At the Water Hole." The squirt gun fight was called "Big Game Hunting." Opening presents and eating birthday cake was actually "The King's Feast." There were more wonderful games and names created by the whole group. They even decided to practice "Animal Charades" with Erin that day so she would know what to do at the real birthday party—besides, it was fun!

Needless to say, both parties were huge successes. I have discovered through many other similar experiences over the years that it is best not to plan FOR the kids, but WITH the kids. Listen to children. They have much to teach adults!

As we went along in school, I remembered what I had learned from Erin and her friends and tried to model that when interacting with educators and other community members. I found that the key was always relationships, relationships, relationships! By connecting with others, we seemed to expand our opportunities to learn and grow and everyone involved benefited from the experience.

Dear Mr. & Mrs. McKenzie,

Thought I'd share a happy observation from the playground. A group of 1st graders were playing 'Follow the Leader' on the Big Toy and Erin was the leader. It was neat. When she started across the bars, Keith called out, "Erin needs help!" Help came.

Have a happy day.

First Grade General Education Teacher

"It is better to listen to children; plan with them, not for them; and honor their ideas by helping make them come true."

Act II – Connecting

Inclusion: It's All About Blue Nail Polish and a Tamagotchi

Original Version Written Summer 1997

It has been seven years since I became a "born-again inclusionist." Our daughter Erin had entered a segregated pre-K program across town that primarily did reverse mainstreaming (first graders coming into the special ed class to play with the students). All of the students were close in age and Erin seemed to be happy. Unfortunately, I wasn't.

That fall I went to the National Down Syndrome Convention in Memphis and heard Marsha Forest, George Flynn, and Barbara Buswell share their visions. I began forming one of my own. A month later I went to a retreat-style conference in Dayton on inclusive education and became completely committed. There have been days in the past seven years that I have felt like I should have been "committed!"

Although our family has received the support of some administrators, teachers, and school personnel, others have shown much consternation and misunderstanding. Every year we have to "sell" our child to someone. We work very hard to ease those minds, and in the end Erin usually wins them over, but it does take its toll.

Just when I am ready to wave the white flag and waiver in my commitment, something happens and I'm reborn. Most recently I have a new resolve because of blue nail polish and a Tamagotchi. Blue nail polish is the color of choice for pre-teen girls, and a Tamagotchi is a "virtual reality pet" also cherished by the same. Erin and her family have been introduced to these important fads by the people who truly understand inclusion best—the kids!

Since Erin began kindergarten at her neighborhood school, her peers have always been calmer and more natural about handling all of this inclusion stuff than we adults. They have figured out creative ways to interact with Erin and have learned to value her for what she has to offer. She is in with the "in" group and with the "out" group and with the group who doesn't care if they're in or out. Erin may not always be a first choice to call or pick, but she is usually the second choice. Her nickname is "E" like the cable channel. She doesn't just participate; she is one of the gang.

The morning that I picked Erin up from the sleepover and found her with her blue nails and her beeping Tamagotchi, this inclusion stuff all made sense again. Erin's friends have assured me that I don't have to worry about Erin going to middle school. For now, I find comfort in that. If only we adults don't screw it up!

"Relationships lead to more opportunities for all."

Reflections of a
Middle School Experience

Original Version Written Spring 2000

The question, "How do people, events, and conditions influence change?" is posted above the blackboard in my daughter's homeroom, also her eighth grade American History classroom. I have been thinking a lot about that question as I have reflected on my recent school visit. Over the last few years at middle school, how have the people Erin has interacted with, and the events, the opportunities, and the educational conditions she has experienced, especially this year, influenced her growth and change? What has changed within her school community? What can we do to make sure positive change continues in her high school community?

In many areas of learning, we have all been surprised by Erin's progress. Who would have guessed:

- How well she would learn to read and continue to learn to read and comprehend.

- How much her reading and comprehension skills would improve by reading the content and vocabulary that she has been exposed to in the general academic classes.

- The knowledge she would acquire in a variety of academic areas—science, social studies, algebra, language arts, and how well she would relate that content to experiences in other settings.

- How responsible she would be in completing her work, following her schedule, not getting lost, and being on time—when she still can't tell time well, does not have the best directional skills, and prefers a lot of other things to "work" as she expresses often.

- That she would figure out supports and cues she needs, and personally advocate for them, and that she would make some very appropriate choices and decisions in some difficult situations—when problem-solving is considered one of her weak areas.

- That she would play soccer and hockey in gym and not get run over!

I am particularly impressed with how unobtrusively support is being given this year. Students often provide more natural supports in a variety of ways. Most importantly, each general education teacher is primarily involved with Erin's learning. The special education teacher provides support by helping to develop modified materials and assignments with each general education teacher.

Sometimes the general education teacher creates these and only needs assistance with reproducing, enlarging, and gathering materials. Everything relates directly to the eighth grade general education curriculum, and the methods Erin uses to present the material support her Individualized Education Program (IEP) goals.

We have never tried consciously to measure the growth of the school community, but I do believe that it has occurred. How have the "people, events, and conditions" surrounding Erin's inclusion affected the whole school community? We'll never know for sure whether they would have occurred regardless, but some of us have noticed that:

- Discussions about "higher level" learning opportunities for *all* students have been taking place.

- We have been thinking about how learning occurs—whether it is only by specific developmental steps and in measurable increments, or it is actually all over the board and requires fewer limits or pre-requisites and more opportunities.

• Folks are looking at how multi-sensory and multiple intelligences approaches can work well for a variety of students.

• Diverse teams representing different perspectives, knowledge, and strengths have become more and more effective, creating opportunities to learn from one another.

We have all been affected in ways we couldn't have predicted.

"How do we discover who is missing and welcome him or her into our community? We have no way of predicting what effect that person or any of us might have on one another."

Act III – Appreciating

Now I'm Brainstorming with My Daughter!

Original Version Written Fall 2000

Over the years, some special education professionals have tried to emphatically point out our daughter's flawed problem-solving skills. To prove their opinions, they have finely detailed five or ten minutes of Erin's life when she didn't have, what they felt, was an appropriate response to a particular problem. When I would suggest another perspective on the situation and Erin's reaction to it, I was thought to be in denial once again. Didn't I realize how much intense, small-group intervention and role-playing Erin needed to practice her decision-making skills? Didn't I know that Erin needed to be protected from her own poor choices in that "safe" special education room?

Yesterday I was riding in the car with my daughter, now a freshman in high school, and she began to talk about an important job she would have that evening as an usher for the school play. Conversational skills have not been one of Erin's strengths and she began to think out loud about what she would say to people when she gave them their programs.

She threw out a few ideas and then asked me what I thought. When she settled on a good welcoming statement, she practiced with herself and then with me. Suddenly I was having one of those "Ah-ha!" experiences. Erin was brainstorming ideas about her communication as well as any speech therapist might and making a thoughtful decision on how best to proceed. Could my daughter possibly be a problem-solver? How did this happen?

Perhaps it began when Erin was first fully included in the neighborhood school kindergarten class and then moved on to first grade with her classmates. The child some special educators were convinced would wander in the school's open-cluster environment never did. The first grade general education teacher didn't realize all of Erin's flaws and just prepared her for the open space along with all the other students.

Maybe it occurred when my daughter hit middle school and had to get organized like all the other students did. There were many classes to attend, a schedule to follow (that changed every other day), and different directions from several different teachers. Her big black notebook with the daily schedule on the front became her most important possession. When Erin had a service club or drama club meeting after school, I would put a sticky note at the end of her schedule to remind her not to come home on the bus. If I forgot to put it there the night before, Erin would remind me that she had a meeting and I needed to get that note done! Since she had to get up so much earlier, clothes planning began the night before. She would carefully select and lay out everything, including socks, shoes and underwear, to put on the next morning.

Erin knew the helpful strategies that worked best for her and made sure they were followed.

It could have happened when Erin got to the high school with 2,000 students. Learning to maneuver in the crowded hallways, find her classes in the huge building, and get to class on time didn't seem to take very long. Erin was on a mission and discovered how to zoom through a crowd with the best of them. She seldom used her locker but instead stuffed everything in her backpack. Guess she learned that from the majority of students who did the same thing. After all, who can get into a locker in a hallway that is wall-to-wall kids and then expect to get anywhere on time?

Of course, I imagine that there are some who would have very different perspectives on these events. Maybe I'll ask Erin what she thinks.

"Let us see the glass as half full rather than half empty and look for the possibilities."

But What About Shakespeare?

Email Note Sent to Two English Teachers in Spring 2003

Dear Peggy and Jim,

Erin attended the State Thespian Conference with the Drama Club this past weekend. I was one of the chaperones. I wanted to share that on Friday night the all-state play was *The Tempest*, and when Erin heard that it was by Shakespeare, she was all excited. She knows him by name. Then on Sunday morning, there was a comedy on the works of Shakespeare where three male characters do short versions (of course made to be outrageously funny) of all of Shakespeare's plays. Erin insisted on attending after she heard that it was about Shakespeare. The actors spent the most time on *Romeo and Juliet* and Erin loved it. But she also got a taste of all the plays.

On Saturday night, we saw one of the best musical presentations I have ever seen, even professionally, of *Les Miserable*. Now, of course, Erin says she has to get the CD. This was her first time to see this play. She was mesmerized, but then we all were—just a phenomenal performance by a high school or any group. Suddenly, at intermission, she said that this was about what she had learned in history and made that connection.

This reinforces for me again the need for all students to be able to access the general education curriculum, even if they can't describe all of the nuances of what they are learning about. I doubt very much that Erin would have gotten any Shakespeare or other great literary pieces in the special ed classroom for students with cognitive and developmental disabilities. That would have been unfortunate. Theatre has also helped Erin to continue to make connections with great literature she has learned about in class. She still watches the *Crucible* all the time—the movie version and a video of Westerville South High School's performance last year.

Please remember this when you are planning for smaller learning communities. All students with any disability label must be part of the mix. Please don't let anyone assume that any student cannot get something out of a lesson.

Thank you both for giving Erin the opportunity to access great literature!

Sincerely,
Barb

"How can any of us decide which opportunities are or are not important in another person's life?"

Reflections on the Journey Toward the VISION for Erin

Abbreviated Version of Several Pages of Observations, Conversations, and Notes Collected During Erin's High School Years from Fall 2000 Through Spring 2004

- Singing and joyfully talking to herself as Erin gets her clothes and book bag ready for school each evening before bed.

- Not getting lost in a huge building with 2,000 students and always getting to class on time.

- Ushering at school plays—and then getting to watch them too.

- Drama Club parties and just hanging out in the L-Way.

- Going to New York with Drama Club and seeing Erin's new favorite play and CD, *Phantom of the Opera*.

- When Erin turned on the bathroom fan and came running out to tell her Dad and me about the air going out of our house, just like she had learned about in ecology that day. Later, she pointed out the humidity in the bathroom because of the steam on the mirror.

- The independent creation of her "commercial" for ecology —"Don't smoke! Yucky, Gross, Ugly! So there!"—that became the creative idea for her science group and the basis for their group commercial.

- "Her interest and enthusiasm has spilled over into the classroom and is a stimulus for other students who see Erin taking her classroom activities so seriously." — ecology teacher

- Being a "Dancing Tree" in the freshman English class mythology play.

- Discovering a love of Shakespeare and being "Juliet" at the Drama Club Halloween party.

- "It is I that am learning so much from Erin. After 22 years of teaching, sometimes it takes a wonderful student like Erin to make us realize why we chose teaching as a profession in the first place." — English teacher

- CAT WITH CLASS Award – "Erin exemplifies all of the characteristics of a true 'Cat with Class.' She is always cheerful and friendly, prepared for her classes, and willing to participate in student activities. She is active in school and community sponsored clubs and events, and demonstrates character traits that make us proud to call her a Westerville South Wild – 'Cat With Class.' " — assistant principal

• Dancing up a storm in gym class! Dancing "Jellicle Ball" from the *CATS* musical for the final.

• Going to the weekend State Thespian Conference with friends from Drama Club.

• Watching the musical *Les Miserable* for the first time and connecting it with something she learned in history.

• Having a summer job at Otterbein College working with the audience services department for their summer theatre as an usher for all of their plays and being invited to continue during the school year.

• "Erin, once again, you've done a wonderful job with this project. I showed your data to my advanced geology class. It helped support a lot of what they've learned about earthquakes. Thank you for allowing me to keep this for a while!" — geology teacher

• "…Teaching Erin has helped me grow as a teacher and person… I've always seen the classroom as very much of a two-way street. I always miss the students when they leave the room, especially at this point in the year. Erin often tells me, "Don't give up," when she sees me pause during a lecture, or express frustration through a sigh when I've misplaced something or other around the room, etc. It always makes me smile. I'll remember her voice, saying those words, in my mind's ear for a long time to come." — geology teacher

- "I was very proud of Erin today. We had a guest speaker who is deaf come in to share her experiences with the ASL class. After she was finished, she asked if the class had any questions. The students were very hesitant, and the few students that asked questions relied on me to interpret (which is fine). Erin raised her hand and asked me if she could "tell her (the speaker) something." I asked Erin if she wanted me to sign for her, or if she would like to sign for herself to which she replied, "Don't worry about it." So I sat back and watched as she signed "Hi, how are you? Are you happy? My name is Erin." I was very impressed not only with her willingness to talk with the guest speaker, but also sign everything for herself! I let her know how proud of her I was, and she said, "It's a piece of cake!" I wish some of my other students would adopt that philosophy!" — American Sign Language teacher

- Being driven to school by friends who are now old enough to drive!

- Erin's excitement when she got her class ring! Wearing it every day.

- Getting her own school jacket with her thespian letter on it.

- Erin getting to stand by one of the microphones at the school choir concert by accident — but taking full advantage of her starring opportunity!

• Giving her "Friends Speech" at conferences in Columbus and at Ohio University and being asked to speak at the International TASH Conference.

• Erin politely asking that others at her IEP meeting speak up so that she could hear them.

• Trying out—singing, acting, and dancing—for *The WIZ*. Choosing to sing "We Shall Overcome" for the singing audition!

• Singing karaoke and dancing to "Get This Party Started" at the Drama Club cast party with friends as back up dancers and everyone cheering Erin on.

• Being recognized by Westerville Parks and Recreation for her outstanding participation on the Youth Commission and in other volunteer activities.

• Being a COOL SENIOR and telling everyone!

• Dancing and partying with special friends.

• Having fun with friends at the senior trip to Cedar Point Amusement Park. Riding EVERY ride, including the really high and really fast roller coasters.

• Getting one of the fun senior awards at the Drama Club banquet—a flashlight with the sign, "Most Likely to Usher on Broadway."

- Being pictured with her class of 2004 and her clubs in the yearbook.

- Getting a thespian medallion to wear for graduation (and then forgetting to wear it like others did!)

- Getting an academic letter.

- Trying out and being selected as one of the seniors giving speeches at the Evening of Reflection and then getting to watch it on the local TV station.

- Getting autographs at the end of the year and friends wishing her luck next year at Otterbein College.

- Phoning friends on her new cell phone that she asked for at graduation.

- Asking friends and family out to lunch and paying with her new credit card.

- Going out to lunch with one of her fellow graduates and her new baby!

- Going to graduation practice and then the real thing. Seeing her picture when she was greeted by the teacher she chose to give her the diploma and the smile that said it all.

• Wanting the same kind of graduation party that her brother had when he graduated but carefully selecting her own menu for the buffet. Being the perfect hostess at HER party.

• Proudly wearing her 2004 necklace everywhere.

"It is important that we take time to observe, reflect, and share what we are learning along the journey toward our vision."

Act IV – Remembering

A Celebration of the Life of Erin

Written and Given at the
Memorial Service by Erin's Friends
August 27, 2004

Kristin Snow: Meghan and I have known Erin since we were little kids in kindergarten. Ever since then, I guess you could say we just couldn't get enough of one another. Throughout elementary school we all experienced many things together like being "letter" people. Then when Emily came in second grade we all had a blast at the haunted gym and helped Erin master the monkey bars and swings. During our time at Annehurst, everyone wanted to be Erin's friend; there wasn't one person who wasn't willing to help. Erin accepted this with open arms. She loved giving out hugs. Everyone knew Erin and she was without a doubt "just one of the girls." One of my favorite things was our infamous sleepovers in her family room where we watched Disney movies, played dress-up, played "pigs in a blanket" and did our makeup and nails. One of her favorite things to do was to watch the movie, *The Mask*, that we got her for her birthday. Our sleepovers were some of the best times we had together. Though we were entering middle school, we knew that nothing would change between us and it could only get better.

Emily Thomas: In middle school, we all went through a change of environment. Even though this was the case, Erin was always there to pick up your spirits in the hall. I can't remember a time when she wasn't happy to see you. At the school dances, or socials as they called them, Erin was there dancing her socks off having a blast. She just never got sick of the music. She also joined the drama club with me and Kristin. She had the opportunity to take a trip to New York City with the drama club, which sparked her love for music even more. Even though we were growing up and taking on new things, we didn't stop having our get-togethers. Every year for Erin's birthday we went out to lunch or dinner and made it a tradition of ours. Erin's favorite place to go was Fujiama where she could interact with the cooks and watch them prepare our meal. We always looked forward to the sparkling pineapple for dessert! We've continued the tradition of getting together with the girls. It was always so fun to go out and catch up on everything. Middle school was filled with memories we'll never forget.

Chelsea Scott: Soon enough it was time for high school. Westerville South was the perfect place for Erin. I had the privilege of meeting Erin my freshman year when we both took choir. She was able to participate in all the activities she liked to do. She loved theatre and was able to be a part of the drama club where she was an usher. Junior year I had history with Erin. Every morning I would come in and no matter what kind of mood I was in she always brought a smile to my face. I sat next to her and got to know her a lot better. Though she sometimes had the help of an aide, she always wanted to make it known how independent she was. I can remember right before a choir concert, if I had a solo, she would always come up to me and give me a hug and tell me that I would do fine and that I was her pal. I am thankful for her acceptance and her willingness to include me in the traditions that were already made. Though I only knew her for a short time, she made an impact on my life, and she will never be forgotten.

Kristin Snow: Erin always went the extra mile in everything she loved to do. One of her favorite hobbies was singing. She took outside voice lessons with Miss Becky and got to perform many solos and we even did a duet together at Christmas time. I was always so amazed at how much confidence Erin exuded. I was always so nervous, but Erin's confidence and passion for music shined through each time, inspiring the audience and making everyone proud. I'm so glad I got to share something so special with Erin.

Meghan Peters: Then came some of my favorite memories with Erin. She was able to go to dances and dance till the wee hours of the night. They allowed her to dress up and hang out with us just like the old days. When I finally got my license I was able to take Erin to school each morning. I personally am not a morning person, but Erin was a different story. Every day when we got in the car, Erin had a new story to share with me. She would talk about her brother and how he was coming home soon or about things in New York he was doing. When he was home she would complain about some little thing he had done, but you knew that she loved more than ever to be able to spend time with him. She would tell me all about things going on with the play coming up or what she was wearing to the next dance. Although the drive was not very long, it was something at least I know I looked forward to every morning. Soon enough our high school times were coming to an end. Towards the end of the year, Erin was able to amaze me once again. At the Night of Reflection, Erin got up on stage and presented a speech she had prepared. She was able to tell all about herself and her experiences. She spoke so clearly and perfectly that it brought me to tears. Then came graduation, Erin had worked hard and had earned herself something wonderful—a high school diploma. As we all prepared to find a college, Erin was able to find herself an opportunity doing something she loved, being part of the theatre at Otterbein College. In the summer, Emily, Kristin, Chelc and I took Erin to her favorite restaurant, Bravo. We had her favorite waiter and it was amazing to see that although she only knew this man from coming to the restaurant, she had touched him in some way. Just like the way she did us, she brought a smile to his face. Things were going great until Chelc spilled her chocolate milk. We soon got over that and had a great time laughing about old times. A few weeks later we decided to go to Bob Evans for breakfast before I left for school. She knew exactly what she wanted, a small orange juice and her eggs and toast. When the waitress came back with a large orange juice Erin was not pleased but as soon as that food came, she was happy as could be. She was not as talkative at this breakfast, but she did talk about how excited she was to go to see Chris in a couple weeks in New York. She was very excited to go and see a play and spend more time with her brother.

Meghan: Erin was not only an inspiration to us but to everyone she met.

Emily: She was high-spirited and was able to make you laugh in the best way.

Chelsea: She touched many people's lives and accomplished so much.

Kristin: It is with no doubt that I say Erin will be truly missed, but will always remain in our hearts and memories forever.

"Belonging does make a difference to everyone involved."

Speech at the 2005 Westerville South Theatre Banquet

Renaming of the Annual Theatre Participation
Award in Erin's Memory

I have met many wonderful people over the years, especially in education, but one that was not so wonderful once said to me that Erin needed to be with her "own kind." I was caught so totally off-guard by such a bigoted and closed-minded comment, that I couldn't even respond. Several years later when I was picking up Erin after her work as an usher at an Otterbein College Theatre performance, I ran into that person. I wanted to say, but I didn't, "By the way, Erin found her 'own kind'—THEATRE LOVERS!"

As a theatre lover myself, I think that the world of drama and musicals can offer great opportunities for all types of diverse individuals and uncover a variety of hidden talents. Sometimes the talent is being a friendly usher who welcomes others in to enjoy; sometimes it is building and painting beautiful sets or sewing interesting costumes or applying colorful makeup;

sometimes it is creating magic with lighting and other technical and backstage feats; sometimes it is dancing and singing on the stage; sometimes it is acting on the stage with or without words; and sometimes it is being an enthusiastic audience participant.

Erin loved everything she did with all of you in theatre here at Westerville South and eagerly participated. Each student who will be recognized tonight with this award that you have generously named in Erin's honor also delights in being with many different kinds of people who just happen to share a love of theatre. These students felt comfortable enough to take risks and begin to discover and share their talents, and these students, in turn, welcomed and encouraged others. My husband and I are so proud to announce the recipients of the Erin McKenzie Theatre Participation Awards.

"Real friendship often comes from our shared interests and passions and not our shared abilities."

Learning Together

My husband and I were trained as educators. I taught for a few years while Gary worked for over 30 years as a teacher and an administrator with Columbus Public Schools. Both of us aspired to be caring teachers and supporters of social justice. After Erin was born, we better understood what that really meant.

We always tried to work as a team with school personnel. To us, an inclusive school community was one where each person, child or adult, was supported to share his or her gifts.

Fortunately we developed relationships with some wonderful educators as both our children went through school. A few of them spoke at the dedication of the Welcoming Space created in memory of Erin in the library of Westerville South High School. It is important to share some of what they learned from Erin.

Pete Swingle, a geology teacher who was chosen by Erin to hand her the diploma at graduation said that he whispered to her that day, "I will never forget you, Erin." At the dedication, he looked up at the spinning dancer in the mural and said at times like this how necessary it becomes for reminders that, "We are all dancing this dance together." Of the eclectic mix of materials and media that were being gathered, he thought, "What a rich resource to discover connections. May we find places where science meets poetry…drama meets nature… math meets music and more…where teachers and beautiful minds can unite."

Peggy Burner, a ninth grade English teacher, became an advocate for Erin as she moved through high school giving advice about academic classes to take that played to Erin's strengths and talking with future teachers. She introduced Erin to Shakespeare, mythology, and *To Kill a Mocking Bird*, among other great literature. Peggy told a wonderful story of when Erin entered her class that fall of freshman year. "On the first day I saw a scared girl…and I realized I was looking in the mirror. I was the one who would be taught so much…things inspired Erin and thus me."

Ann Fowble was the special educator who became an inclusion facilitator. We were fortunate to have Ann with us from the time Erin was in kindergarten through high school graduation. She traveled to conferences with me and we also co-presented to a variety of audiences. Ann had the benefit of that long relationship and offered her observations at the dedication. She felt that the Welcoming Space was, "a wonderful way to share the gifts that Erin shared." Ann identified those gifts as a love of learning to read, which allowed Erin to read her speeches and speak publicly; appreciating our gifts, "Erin knew she was different but never thought of herself as less than anyone else"; and creating a sense of community around her. Teachers would say to her, "The year I had Erin in my class, I had the most exceptional group of students."

Michele Fuchs, an 11th and 12th grade film and literature teacher, recommended that the space be dynamic with a variety of media to honor Erin's energetic learning style and approach to life. Her favorite, almost daily greeting from Erin was "Hey, girl!" Michele felt that, "Film and Literature was the perfect course for Erin because she loved the performing arts… She loved *Hamlet* and her enthusiasm inspired the class." Michele shared that she was also uneasy at first, "but I too discovered that Erin was going to teach me. The atmosphere of the class was better because Erin was there."

Assistant Principal Barry Ackerman concluded, "We try to bring the best out in our students. Erin brought the best out in us."

"The importance of connecting and learning with one another cannot be overemphasized."

Opening the Door to College

Can we learn to be inclusive in an exclusive environment? On college and university campuses we talk about how to teach students with labels or work with people with disabilities, and there are few, if any, present to be part of the conversation. We talk *about*, not *with*. How can we learn about inclusion without experiencing it?

Inclusion advocate Norm Kunc has addressed the challenge of trying to create inclusive communities within typically competitive elementary, middle, and high school cultures. The philosophy of the entire school must become more mutually supportive to truly welcome all and for all to benefit. In spite of some progress that has been made at the K-12 level, postsecondary education has yet to embrace inclusion. Rather than trying to figure out how to support each student to attend college classes and participate in campus activities, many segregated programs are being developed in misguided attempts to get students with disabilities onto college campuses.

We were not interested in Erin becoming a member of a special education class on a college campus. As she got closer to high school graduation, we tried a different approach.

I wanted to introduce the idea of college to Erin in a way that might interest her. Her first impression of college was not a good one. Her brother had gone away to Ohio University, and she missed him. Erin had no desire to leave home. Fortunately there was a wonderful college right in our city of Westerville. Once we started to develop relationships with people at Otterbein College, Erin began to view the idea of going to college with more enthusiasm.

Erin loved the theatre and was an active member of Thespian Troop 513 in high school. Through a friend in the Otterbein Education Department, we made a connection with the Theatre Department's director of audience services. Erin started ushering the summer before her senior year and was asked to continue all that year and into the next summer. She made friends, was in an area that interested her, and began to understand more about what the college experience could be.

Following high school graduation, her job with the Theatre Department was going to be expanded. We were talking about Erin taking classes. This was possible only because of the relationships she had formed within the Otterbein community.

We never got to see where this journey would take us, but we did get some glimpses after Erin's passing. We received many kind wishes and personal notes from Otterbein students and faculty, some we knew and some we had not met before. All revealed what Erin's presence and involvement had meant to them. A recent graduate living and acting in New York City wrote, "Erin's love and passion for theatre were inspiring. Seeing her usher and watch these shows that have become the norm in my life—her excitement and joy always showing—it brought a new light to our theatre and helped renew my love."

"Systems and institutions do not include; a community of people includes."

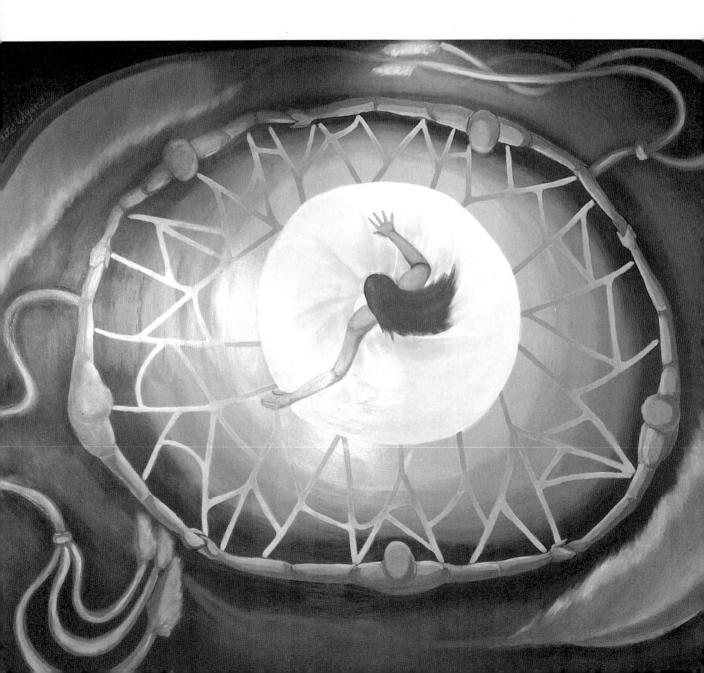

Epilogue:
Spinning in Community with Others

Erin's life inspired the creation of the Welcoming Space in the Library of Westerville South High School and the Erin McKenzie Virtual Welcoming Space Web site at Otterbein College Courtright Memorial Library. Both provide a diverse mix of media styles and information to encourage conversations and facilitate our discovery of one another's cultures, experiences, and how we are connected; celebrate the gifts and talents in each of us; and help us to build inclusive communities where all are valued.

The mural on the wall of the high school library's space was inspired in part by an article my friend Candee found about the Whirling Dervishes of Turkey. The spinning of the dancer is an intentional act of participation in what is believed to be the shared similarity and revolution of all other beings.

Student artist Sarah Boatright took that theme and combined it with the significance of the circle in Native American culture to create a beautiful painting of a young woman with long, flowing hair who looks very much like Erin spinning within a dream catcher. On a wall to the side are the words, "Mitakuye Oyasin," which is taken from the Lakota/Dakota language and can be translated, "We are all related," or "All my relations." It is a belief of oneness and harmony with the universe.

This connection was also important to Erin. My husband was involved for many years with the central Ohio Native American community. When we attended events, Erin was always genuinely welcomed and invited to dance in the circle.

Sarah's artwork has marvelously captured how two very different cultures celebrate the importance of community. Erin's life powerfully demonstrated that too.

May we all spin happily together.

"Celebrate our humanity that connects us."

Visit the Erin McKenzie Virtual Welcoming Space at:
http://library.otterbein.edu/ErinMcKenzie/index.htm

View a video of Erin giving one of the senior speeches at the 2004
Westerville South High School Evening of Reflection at:
http://library.otterbein.edu/ErinMcKenzie/video.htm